# What Makes You Happy?

Written by Charnan Simon • Illustrated by Jan Bryan-Hunt

Published in the United States of America by The Child's World®
PO Box 326 • Chanhassen, MN 55317-0326
800-599-READ • www.childsworld.com

**Reading Adviser**

Cecilia Minden-Cupp, PhD, Former Language and Literacy Program Director,
Harvard Graduate School of Education, Cambridge, Massachusetts

**Acknowledgments**

The Child's World®: Mary Berendes, Publishing Director

Editorial Directions, Inc.: E. Russell Primm, Editorial Director and Project Manager; Katie Marsico,
Associate Editor; Judith Shiffer, Assistant Editor; Caroline Wood, Editorial Assistant

The Design Lab: Kathleen Petelinsek, Design and Art Production

**Library of Congress Cataloging-in-Publication Data**

Simon, Charnan.
    What makes you happy? / written by Charnan Simon ; illustrated by Jan Bryan-Hunt.
        p. cm. — (Magic door to learning)
    Summary: Illustrations and simple rhyming text show some of the ways family members can
be happy.
    ISBN 1-59296-623-3 (library bound : alk. paper)
    [1. Happiness—Fiction. 2. Family life—Fiction. 3. Stories in rhyme.] I. Bryan-Hunt, Jan, ill.
II. Title. III. Series.
    PZ8.3.S5874Wha 2006
    [E]—dc22                          2006001407

A book is a door, a magic door.
It can take you places
you have never been before.
Ready? Set?
Turn the page.
Open the door.
Now it is time to explore.

What makes you happy?
Are you like me?
I like warm days . . .

6

and cold nights . . .

7

familiar faces . . .

and brand-new sights.

My Grandma
likes to garden,
and my Grandpa
likes to dance.

Mom and Dad like
to cook together
whenever they
have a chance.

My brother likes
to read a book.
My sister likes to hike.

My puppy? Well,
there's nothing
my happy puppy
doesn't like!

What makes me happy?

I start to count and then—I get so many happy thoughts, I have to start again!

NATURE

WALKING TRAILS

HiKing

BUGS

Book of Birds

23

Our story is over, but there is still much to explore beyond the magic door!

What do you do on days when you're not happy? How about creating a rainy-day poster to cheer you up? Use a ruler and markers to divide a piece of poster paper into ten sections. In each section, draw a picture of someone or something that makes you happy. You can look at your poster when you're sad, angry, or upset. It will remind you of all the wonderful things that make you smile. Share your poster with family and friends—it might cheer them up, too!

These books will help you explore at the library and at home:

Boynton, Sandra. *My Puppy Book.* New York: Workman Publishers, 2005.

Lee, Spike, Tonya Lewis Lee, and Kadir Nelson (illustrator). *Please, Puppy, Please.* New York: Simon & Schuster for Young Readers, 2005.

## About the Author

Charnan Simon lives in Madison, Wisconsin, where she can usually be found sitting at her desk and writing books, unless she is sitting at her desk and looking out the window. Charnan has one husband, two daughters, and two very helpful cats.

## About the Illustrator

Jan Bryan-Hunt is a freelance illustrator living near Kansas City with her husband and two children. Spending time with her family, taking walks on a sunny day, and creating stuff in her studio is what makes her happy.